The Art of Mystery Shopping

By

Sandy Schauer

Montanita Publishing
P.O. Box 1054 Los Lunas NM 87031
Copyright 2014 by Montanita Publishing
ISBN-13: 978-1497521070

Contents

The Opening

You've been looking for a way to make a little bit of money. You've heard about mystery shopping. You Google mystery shopping and find a myriad of stories that tout how easy mystery shopping is. Then you find the websites for mystery shopping companies. Wow, you may not make much money performing a job, but no tax will be taken out of what you earn and you'll be on your own. Sounds like a great way to put cash in your pocket.

Wait! Mystery shopping isn't always glamorous, nor is it

sometimes that easy. And there are a variety of hidden costs that must be figured into the monetary equation.

For the uninitiated, mystery shopping is most often just what it sounds like — walking or driving into an establishment as a customer and making a purchase/request/order just as any customer would do.

In the years I have mystery shopped, my jobs have included:

• Eating. Restaurants are among the major mystery shopping participants. Large chain fast food restaurants need to be shopped with regularity, as do other eateries.

• Blowing up balloons with helium, placing them in store aisles, and returning weekly to restock and report the number of balloons.

• Photographing signs in movie theaters. This assignment included checking the volume level in individual auditoriums.

• Visiting a big box retailer to find out if a particular laundry detergent endcap (the end of the aisle) is set on the sales floor. If it was not set up then I was to locate and place the display.

• Laying my body on mattresses at a company with many outlets in the community.

• Walking through office supply stores checking on the status of printers, inks, and photo papers manufactured by a major company.

• Asking a teller at a credit union if I could perform a financial transaction there since I was not near my own credit union. I successfully conducted the transaction.

• Placing hangtag coupons on bottles of laundry detergent at a big box retailer. This job would have included locating the detergent and putting it on the shelves if store personnel had not already done so.

• Counting prepaid telephone cards, as well as gift cards, on racks at dollar stores. In addition, I checked the cell phones on display for missing or damaged parts.

• Assembling a magazine rack and then placing the magazines on the rack.

• Placing new signage on a baby high chair. This task was easy in one store because the chair was on the floor. In another store the high chair had been placed on a pedestal so that I needed a ladder. I found a store ladder and was doing my job when a manager walked by and expressed displeasure. I wasn't an employee and I was using a company ladder performing what could have been a dangerous task. He was not happy and I will not perform such acrobatics again.

• Changing out the identification tags on the shelves below household products. This involved stripping out the old tags and putting new ones on. I was very careful on this assignment because the products were alike except for the length. I didn't want to label a fifty-foot package of aluminum foil as twenty-five feet.

• Taking photographs of and assessing the condition of the meat department in a big box grocery store. This was a covert assignment so I felt very strange standing in the store aisle taking pictures, hoping no one would ask what I was doing. I wasn't sure I would have a believable story to give if someone questioned me.

• Replacing posters in frames on walls and replenishing brochures.

• Checking whether sandwich racks and sandwiches had been placed in the delicatessen department of a big box store.

• Placing stickers on children's toys in a big box store.

Basics You Need To Start

You will apply to shop for different companies on a computer and you will make your reports using a computer so you will need a computer of one type or another. Some companies accept reports by Smartphone, but you may find that you want to read instructions or search out shopping information using a laptop or desktop computer because it will be easier on your eyes.

Transportation to get to your shops is very important. In rural areas you will probably use a car. A transportation system in urban areas may allow you to get easily from place to place without a vehicle. You may be able to schedule several shops in a mall, but before you plan your route through the mall to your stores, you must first get to that shopping mall.

Other items that will help you get your jobs done include a printer/scanner, cell phone, digital camera, and stopwatch or a stopwatch app on your Smartphone.

You must know how to operate all these items before you can be a successful mystery shopper. And you should be handy with them so that the accomplishment of your shop is not impeded by your inability to use your phone or scan your receipt. Being able to handle your equipment and transportation will also increase your earning ability.

Read on for more information about many of the items just mentioned.

Photographs and Scanning

Some mystery shopping instructions call for a digital camera. I think that means a camera rather than a Smartphone. With the high quality of Smartphone cameras it's possible to use a Smartphone for shops. But if the company specifically says use a digital camera then I will use a camera.

Photos or scans of receipts and sending those photos/scans along with the report are an integral part of mystery shopping. The receipt proves you were at the site. Without the receipt you will not get paid. You may know you are honest and that you would not report a shop unless you performed that shop. The mystery shopping company hiring you has no idea of your honesty and needs that receipt.

Receipts are easily lost or even thrown away. You lay your receipt on the tray your meal was served on and then have it slide under the extra napkins. When you finish eating, you empty your trash into the bin and place the tray on top of the counter. Into the bin went your receipt, the proof of your shop. If you do this a few times and end up not getting paid for your food and your time then you may have learned to put that receipt somewhere safe as soon as possible.

The photo or scan of your receipt needs to be legible and readable. The report checker may well match the receipt with your report to be sure the times make sense. The times may not exactly match. The clock on the business's cash register may not be the time on your cell phone or wristwatch. But there should not be a great difference between the time you say you arrived and the time on the receipt. If you say you arrived at 5:15 p.m. then the receipt should not say 6:30 p.m.

Don't spill food on your receipt, especially don't spill food so the receipt can't be read. Don't cut off the name of the business, address, or anything else on that piece of paper. If the receipt is too long to fit on your scanner then cut it in half and place the two pieces of paper on the scanner. Some mystery shopping companies say they will accept a mailed receipt, but this is so antiquated I'm sure employees laugh when someone does use the United States Postal Service.

Scanners are relatively inexpensive and easy to use. If you must, you can take a photograph of your receipt and email that. The scanner usually flattens the receipt if it has become scrunched. When you are photographing a receipt that has been crushed and does not lay flat then try to flatten it. The wavy part might be the total you want to be reimbursed. If someone cannot read the amount then it will be difficult to pay you.

Computers Are Necessary

I'm a Mac/Apple user, have been almost three decades. I've run a business for many years so my husband and I upgrade the computers when necessary. The shops I performed for one company had been sent in using the Safari browser on my Mac computer for almost a year and a half. No questions asked, no lost reports.

When my reports suddenly did not go through I was told I could only send in reports using Internet Explorer. Well, my up-to-date operating system will not run Internet Explorer. The company is working on a more compatible system, but until such a system is in place on their website I cannot perform any jobs.

This company had a grading system for shoppers. My grade was 4.9 out of a possible five. I always received glowing reviews of my shops. I liked performing the shops for this company because they were more interesting than others and often did not involve food with lots of calories.

So I went searching for another company that would not shut out part of the population from doing a good job.

Whatever computer operating system you use, when you fill out the shop reports you will find that you may need to be extra careful because you cannot save the report as you go along. Many people are inveterate savers, pushing the requisite keys every few minutes so they don't have to redo any work. This is a good habit.

But if the report does not have the capacity of being saved then make sure you don't accidentally close the file because whatever you did will probably disappear and you will need to start over. In some cases the answers are automatically saved to the report even if you don't push the button so that the information doesn't have to be re-entered if the report closes for some reason.

Mystery Shopping Tidbits

When you first think of mystery shopping, you might believe you can go to any shopping mall, pick and choose what stores you want to shop, visit those stores to make purchases without any instructions, and then get reimbursed for your purchases. Mystery shopping works somewhat like this description, but not really.

Businesses hire companies who hire people, generally as independent contractors, who then mystery shop. And specific rules must be followed when mystery shopping with different guidelines for different businesses.

Mystery shopping companies are numerous, some have been around for decades, others are relatively new. When you search for companies to work for, you may not be able to find out what businesses a mystery shopping company handles until you sign up with that company.

Signing up is relatively easy. There's the basic information to fill in – name, address, phone number. This may be followed by questions about preferences that relate to the mystery shops the company assigns. Perhaps the company works with several fast food restaurants. There might be a question about food allergies or dietary restrictions.

Some mystery shopping companies want to know if you have or are shopping for other companies. They may request you list those companies. Narratives may be called for so applicants are asked to write about specific situations. I'm a writer by trade and can produce a narrative easily. Others may not be able to write the narrative and will not be hired to perform shops that include this task.

A few composite websites exist which list mystery shopping jobs available within certain zip codes. These could show the pay available for the shop, an amount that may come as a shock because mystery shopping does not always pay very well.

The preliminary offered rate for some jobs may sound decent and fair, especially when you add the food reimbursement. But jobs sometimes take longer than anticipated. They take longer because it's difficult to figure out instructions written by someone else, because the address does not include a street direction such as northeast or southwest, and because a not-paid-for "precall" must be made.

Mystery shopping assignments can be very detailed. Unless one has an eidetic memory it may be necessary to print the instructions. No big deal. Except that printing anything from a computer costs money. How much it costs depends on the price of the printer and the price of that cartridge or toner in the printer.

I performed a job to check on inventory of a vacuum cleaner brand at a big box retailer and printed thirty pages for that one job. About a third of the pages had very little information so the ink use was minimal. Other pages had the standard amount of information.

A very few mystery shopping companies reimburse for printing. When I discovered one company that provided that payment I wanted to cheer. At last, people who understood a cost was involved in producing the supplies needed to do the job.

Because the shops can be very detailed, it can take time to figure out how to accomplish the shop. Instructions may need to be read and reread for a complete understanding of the task. All this takes time, time that needs to be figured into the cost of accomplishing any job.

There is, of course, the expense of getting to the site. A shopper should not take on driving an hour, seventy miles perhaps, for a payment of twenty dollars. That is tantamount to paying the mystery shopping company for the pleasure of working. A shop might be a distance from the shopper's home or office, but on the way to somewhere else the shopper is going. This could still make the job somewhat profitable.

Inputting information into the computer should be figured into the time needed for a shop. And that time can be multiplied by any number of unexpected circumstances. Some companies do not have a save key for their forms. Not having a save key is quite scary. A glitch can happen to a computer system halfway through filling out a form and erase your work, which has not been saved. That means whatever was keyboarded has to be keyboarded again.

A company form may not go through to be registered as turned in. No telling how something like that happens, but it can. If the form has been saved along the way and can be accessed again then all is well and good. A non-saved form may need to be filled in (again).

Sending photographs with reports can be tricky and time consuming. A jpeg is a jpg, or so I thought, until one company's system would only take my jpgs, not jpegs. Some computer programs produce a jpeg. Some reports prefer jpgs. A jpeg can be exported to become a jpg.

Picture sizes are important in the computer world and for reports. Some mystery shopping companies have a program that is part of their reporting process that facilitates sending pictures. Other reports count on the mystery shopper having the ability to figure out how to send pictures.

Finally, in the jobs I held previous to mystery shopping, I often had to perform tasks I didn't want to do. I'd clench my teeth or make myself think positively and barrel my way through the task until completed. The nice thing about mystery shopping is you have the choice of doing what you want to do. That's good because you may find that once you have done a shop for one particular company you may not want to perform that task or work for that company again.

Mystery Shopping Keeps Evolving

One mystery shopping company I worked with evolved their business into conducting what were termed business verifications which involved going to businesses, asking detailed questions of a specific person at the business, and taking photographs.

I had no clue what necessitated the interview and pictures. When I called and set up the appointment to meet with the specific someone at the business, I read from a script. That script included the name of the company I performed the work for and the firm that hired that company. The people I interviewed often recognized the names.

The business verifications were performed for different companies so the questions changed, although the photographs pretty much stayed the same. The companies ranged from used car dealerships to large airplane builders to home-based businesses, and many types of businesses in-between.

The questionnaire could also be very basic with no people contact or complex with pictures of all the rooms (including bathrooms) in the interior and pictures of every side of the exterior plus other outside photos in addition to an extensive questionnaire. The in-between was about six pictures and a short questionnaire.

Business verifications earned more money, perhaps because they involved taking pictures. Sometimes they proved more interesting. I enjoyed visiting the businesses and talking to the people. The business verifications might not even be called mystery shopping, except the company I started with as a shopper took them on as part of their business.

When one mystery shopping company purchased another, I began working for the new company, but where mystery shopping had been the focus for the first company, the second did a lot of merchandising. The merchandising jobs consisted mainly of going into stores and changing the locations of items and/or moving items.

The first time I performed a merchandising job it involved five separate shelf areas where products had to be moved around and about. And the strips detailing what was on each shelf had to be removed and replaced. It took me what seemed like forever on that first job. And it involved a lot of physical exercise, up and down, even sideways, as I pushed and shoved the products around.

I was assigned several stores and, with each one, the job became easier, but those five changes were still a lot of work. It was tough way to break into merchandising. I spent several months performing these jobs. Some consisted of only a few changes. Others were exhausting as they included moving and rearranging many shelves.

Multiple Shops That Are The Same

Mystery shopping companies may contract to shop at, or even inspect, businesses with multiple sites. This results in similar or the same shops at many locations within an area, municipality, or state. A shopper can sign up for several shops that will be identical, or sometimes almost. This can be both good and bad.

The good is that once you've done one shop then each succeeding shop is easier because you know what the questions are and what photographs must be taken. Or you know what the basic tasks are. The bad is that it's easy to become confused and send the wrong photographs or information for the locations. Or even confuse the tasks by starting to do something that was not assigned to one store, but assigned to others. Then you will be wasting your time.

The people who check the reports before sending them on to the corporations wanting them will insist the shopper send the correct pictures or make the changes necessary to the report. So care must be taken to be sure the information and pictures match each individual site. Or that you did exactly what is required.

I'm a fan of multiple shops. It can be much easier doing multiple shops. I feel secure performing multiple shops as long as I pay attention to the instructions.

An international manufacturer of products sold in office supply stores, as well as other outlets, wants to know how those products are displayed. There may be ten outlets in a large city. The questions are the same for every outlet. The jobs don't pay that much, but if you bunch the sites then you make some money. You can cut down on expenses by printing the form once and filling it out with different color ink. Before you do that, make absolutely sure the form is not different for different outlets.

If you want to save money on printing, but don't want to use the same sheet for more than one business then you can print two sheets to a page. The pages will be half the size, and you may have to squint, but it's workable.

Some stores may restrict visits by vendors. And you are considered a vendor in many people's thoughts and actions. The restrictions may be that you cannot visit the store during certain hours. I follow the directions when the instructions say, "Do not go to Office Support between the hours of noon and four p.m." Sometimes I wait a few minutes in my car to be sure I don't hit the wrong time.

You may not get paid if you chose not to follow these instructions. The report checkers look at the receipts just as they look at the reports. They will know what times are forbidden and will send you an email telling you that you will not be paid because you were in the store when you should not have been.

Sometimes You're Graded

Somebody does read the reports, check the information, verify the receipts, and look at the pictures. Somebody has to because mystery shoppers are not infallible. Mystery shoppers send duplicate photos, don't catch misspellings in narratives, or fail to get a specific photograph. The checker's job is to make sure the report fills the needs of the corporation wanting them, and, if it doesn't, get back with the shopper for changes.

A few companies grade reports. The shopper receives an email saying the report is satisfactory or, perhaps unsatisfactory, or even excellent, and is assigned a grade; say nine out of ten possible points. On the home page the shopper accesses when checking out job possibilities, that shopper's overall score shows up. At the top of the page might be the sentence "You have performed 33 shops since (the date the shopper started)" and then "Your shopper score is a 9.5 out of a possible 10."

Food and Food Timing

Food in one form or another is a big part of mystery shopping and so are calories. One of the best-known hamburger joints requires shoppers order a meal from the drive-through and the walk-in restaurant in the same mystery shop. Each of these lunch or dinner shops involves ordering a starch such as fries, as well as a form of a burger or chicken, generally with a bun. The instructions are very specific about what can be ordered and no salads are listed. This may be caused by the fact that the mystery shop is centered on what is ordered by the majority of the customers, often not the healthiest or leanest choices.

Mystery shops have to be focused on the product ordered by most people. If the majority wants a hamburger on a bun with fries then why find out how long it takes to deliver that healthy salad? People will keep coming back for the hamburger and its companions if those products taste good, are delivered in a timely fashion, and are priced right.

But being a mystery shopper can mean adding on the pounds unless one is careful. Tater tots with a sausage sandwich for breakfast, and burgers or hot dogs with buns accompanied by fries for lunch, may necessitate a very skimpy salad with no dressing for dinner.

Burger and hot dog joints are not the only eating places mystery shopped. Many restaurants are shopped, but it is not always easy to find the company that will hire you to visit a restaurant that offers healthier or leaner choices.

When you find a casual, or even elegant, restaurant to shop then you need to, once again, read the instructions carefully because all types of conditions must be followed. You may be able to buy a meal for yourself and a companion, but you will need to order two different entrees. This makes absolute sense. The restaurant executives want to know how the chefs prepare various entrees.

Many fast food shops are one-person shops and the instructions say the shoppers should be alone, no children, no spouse, no one else. Casual or fancy restaurant shops can be for two people, with each ordering something different. I've not done many fancy restaurant shops, but I did take my husband along on one that cured us of ever wanting to go into that restaurant again.

The food at the restaurant was good, the service excellent, but the noise extreme. We could not hear each other talking. The good food was served in a hit-and-miss style with servers coming along with different types of meat cut directly on the dinner plate. Sounds okay, except that it seemed more like a buffet than a sit-down dinner. Neither my husband nor I are fond of buffet-style dining. I gave the restaurant a decent report because the food was good and the service excellent. I didn't want to take our particular likes or dislikes out on the business. Since our one time there I've received numerous emails announcing a shop at the location, but I have no interest in returning alone or with someone.

Timing is everything in mystery shopping. Most food shops require at least one time written in the report and often that is the beginning time. With food preparation the minutes and seconds between ordering and receiving food is very important. Also necessary to record may be the minutes and seconds between arriving in a line and placing the order or the time between pushing a button at a drive-through and a worker asking for your order.

Different food establishments are concerned about different timings. That's why it's important, once again, to read the instructions. The requirements are usually spelled out very clearly, and often, many times. The timing is not just in minutes, but also seconds. Be careful about using zeros and fives when reporting times because that may indicate not tracking the time, but making it up.

Do You Want To Pay For Training?

There isn't much training involved in mystery shopping, but once in a while, training might be necessary to help with a job that occurs on a regular basis. I was one of many mystery shoppers across the nation stocking a specialty item every week at a name brand big box retailer. A change in the delivery mode necessitated training about how to get the specialty item on the shelves. The mystery shopping company provided the training, but the shoppers had to spend two unpaid hours taking the training by dialing into a non-toll-free line. Wow, unpaid time and the expense of a long distance phone call. This for a job barely paying a minimum wage for the sixty to ninety minutes every week to perform the task.

Sometimes decisions have to be made and the one about this training was easy. Resentment overwhelmed me about the time and cost so I emailed saying I couldn't participate. It wasn't a lie, but it wasn't a truth. Maybe if the call had been toll free then I might not have resented the time. Maybe if payment had been offered for my time then I would have gladly dialed the phone number. The cost of the phone call and the two hours for the class with no pay said there was little concern about shoppers. This project folded not too long after the training because it involved a product that became no longer available.

Another company offered $2.50 to take training before performing an inventory job. The test was easy to take. The company's website included an area called "eknowledge." I clicked on that to find the tests for several businesses. I located the one I was interested in, took the test, and passed.

Most mystery shopping companies try to work with their contractors. Those that don't are the ones that shoppers don't stay with.

The World We Live In

Mystery shopping assignments can be impacted by world or national events. I took on an assignment to fill balloons once a week at a big box retailer and place those balloons for sale in the aisles. My instructions said I couldn't spend more than seventy-five minutes on the first assignment. Well, I could spend more time, but I would not be paid for more than the seventy-five minutes at just slightly better than minimum wage.

That first time the task took much longer than the allotted time because I had to figure out where the materials were located, discuss with managers where the balloons would be displayed, and organize the project for the future. After that everything went well for several months. The employees recognized me, greeting me as I performed my duties. I spent an hour a week at the store, just as my instructions said I should be doing.

Then the national crisis of a diminishing helium supply impacted my job.

When I started the project the big box retailer had three gigantic bottles of helium. Store personnel used the helium to blow up balloons to attract customers to buy products. I used the helium to blow up balloons to be sold. One day the store totally ran out of helium.

Nearly a month passed until a filled bottle of helium appeared in the store. During that time I talked to a number of store personnel about ordering helium. I made weekly trips to nag. My payments were supposed to be for filling balloons. I didn't get paid for traveling to the store to nag or filling out the numerous forms that announced the helium had not yet arrived.

The new bottle of helium didn't seem to last that long, but then I had worked with three bottles when I first started. It took more than a month for another bottle to appear and all too quickly the gas was used up. I tried to tell the big box employees how to order the helium in the most expeditious way, using instructions passed on to me by the people I worked for.

Nothing happened for weeks and weeks and then my job of blowing up balloons was canceled. I'll never know if the cancellation was because my particular big box employees couldn't figure how to order the helium or because it became too much trouble nationwide to continue. Nor will I ever know if the people who created the balloon project had a clue that told them helium would be in short supply as the company tried to create a market for their balloons.

Those Ego-Smashing Negatives

Mystery shopping companies offer different jobs because the businesses they work for want different information or because the needs change as time goes by. One of my first jobs was purchasing at least three items at a grocery store. I would then be reimbursed up to nine dollars for the items plus a five-dollar payment for my work.

The tasks included inspecting specific areas of the store, dealing with at least three employees, and making sure one of the items was left on the bottom of the cart (to know if the cashier would find this item before finishing checkout). I performed this shop many times. About six months after I started, the grocery chain decided that this particular form of mystery shopping was not giving them the information they needed and stopped the jobs.

A few months after discontinuing the shops, the grocery chain's executives decided to conduct surveys in the stores. Not every store and not very often. The description of the job made it sound easy and it paid much better than most mystery shops. And there was a reason it paid better – the job was not that easy and was filled with ego-smashing nos.

The surveys had to do with the in-store advertising for a credit card issued by the grocery store. My job was to stand near the cash registers and convince exiting shoppers to stop and answer a three-to-five minute survey. I could give every person who answered the full survey two dollars. Problem was I had to get them to stop to hear my pitch. Then I had a set of qualifiers before the survey could even be posed to a possible participant.

People were very nice. Really, they were. But I'm not always good with a negative response, even if it isn't intended as an insult to me. People would give me long stories about why they couldn't take the time to answer the survey, long stories that took the same amount of time as answering the questions.

And then I would finally have someone say, "Yes, I'd love to answer your survey" and they would start responding to the qualifying questions. Sure enough, one of their answers would prevent them from helping me finish my job. As the day wore on, when someone become disqualified I felt the urge to just pass over that special question to let them finish the survey. I couldn't do it. I'm too honest even if I wanted to get my job done. Even if I didn't want to hear one more person's tale about why they couldn't spend time with the survey.

I'd never done survey work in public before and I'm not sure I want to do it again. Maybe if I took the "nos" less as a personal insult then I would do fine. Maybe if I realized that people really didn't have the time for the survey, but wanted someone to hear their tale of woe then I would do it again. Maybe if I'm asked in a moment of forgetting the nos then I might agree to be a survey taker somewhere, but it won't be any time soon.

How Do I Get Paid?

When you sign on to perform a mystery shop, the amount you'll be paid is generally listed somewhere easy to find. Sometimes you can wait out the companies so they pay you more because no one has taken the shop on and the job has to be done in that month.

Mystery shopping companies not only hire report checkers, but also independent contractors, or sometimes employees, who call shoppers to urge them to perform a shop. Sometimes the contractors/employees try to convince the shopper to work for the measly amount listed on the website. Other times these people offer a more substantial amount.

Mystery shopping is certainly not going to make you rich. In fact the monthly income may pay your cell phone bill. It is more fun than some other jobs and even pays better than some jobs if you know what you are doing.

Payment for mystery shopping is as varied as the tasks. Some companies pay twice a month via direct deposit in a very short time. I love these companies because the payment is quick and almost immediate. But then there are the companies that use PayPal that don't pay until the next month after the shop. This means that you could do a job in the first week of January and not have the money in your PayPal account until nearly the end of February. It's an awfully long time to wait, but these companies announce up front they conduct business in this manner and payment is not made until the month following the month when the job is performed.

And there are still companies that pay the old-fashioned way — with a check. These companies may pay more quickly than those that use PayPal, but the shopper now has to deposit that check into an account or cash the check before having the money.

Mystery shoppers have no choice in the payment mechanism. You take it as it is offered, no negotiation, no possible change in the cycle. It is what they offer and nothing else. And if you end up performing jobs for companies that pay twice a month via direct deposit then be grateful you see the money so quickly.

Some companies may pay more quickly because they ask shoppers to invest their own money in the job. A shop may involve rewarding employees for how they perform their jobs. The reward will be cash out of the mystery shopper's pocket. For instance, the shopper is assigned the task of ordering specific food items, and seeing if the order taker performs certain tasks at a fast food restaurant.

If the order taker accomplishes his job correctly, the shopper congratulates him with money along with an explanation of what he did to earn the cash. If the order taker did not do as the trainers taught him to do then he gets a piece of paper that says he needs to figure out how to do his job right.

So the shopper is out the money for the food and the money given to the order taker, which may well be three times as much as the food. This might be why some companies pay more often – mystery shoppers are investing their money in the rewards for a job well done.

I've worked as an independent contractor and I've paid people as independent contractors. Never did I take payments for workers' compensation out of the checks I issued. But one company I worked for did just that. A set percentage (very minimal) was deducted from the checks for workers' compensation.

Workers' compensation is a form of insurance providing wage replacement and medical benefits to employees injured in the course of employment in exchange for mandatory relinquishment of the employee's right to sue his or her employer for the tort of negligence. This definition is from Wikipedia. Note that it mentions employees.

It was made clear to me when I signed up with this company that I was an independent contractor. It was also made clear that funds would be deducted for workers' compensation. I was given no option. When the checks arrived, they clearly showed the money taken out. (And yes, this large company with hundreds, probably thousands, of independent contractors did mail checks rather than using direct deposit.)

Those Pesky Instructions

At this stage in my life I think I am good at reading instructions. Maybe I'm not. Or perhaps I just skip over the important parts of information. Or maybe it's that I think I remember what's in the instructions, but then something happens during the job that's slightly different. I should reexamine the instructions but I don't. What's the result? I end up doing extra work. Extra work I won't be paid for even at the lowly rate mystery shoppers earn.

The lesson learned is to take the time to read the instructions several times. And then read them again when something different happens that impacts the job. One job I performed involved counting DVDs in general merchandise stores. When I was at my last stop of a very long day, I located a box of DVDs in the back storeroom rather than on display in the store.

In my report I said I found the box, but did not count the DVDs. When I say count, I mean having a list of titles and marking each title with how many are in the store.

I ended up going back to this store, which was far away from my home base, to count the DVDs in the box because that was in the instructions. I had not read the instructions (again) before I left the parking lot or even reread them before I filled out the report form.

I went back because the shop checker emailed that the instructions specifically stated a shopper must count the titles in any box of DVDs and add that count to the number on display. I could have made the numbers up and just added them to the report. I figure that making up information comes back to the person creating the fantasy. And I know that it's easy to get tangled up in lies, even those lies that result in not traveling many miles to do what should have been done in the first place.

I had done the DVD job several times and it seemed simple. I had never found a box that remained in a storeroom because workers didn't feel they had the space to add inventory. I didn't check my instructions to read about what to do with the box.

Mystery shopping instructions are pretty straightforward and make sense, most of the time. Yet there can be a problem because someone writes the instructions without having to perform them. The instructions may make sense on paper, but could be difficult to accomplish.

Before starting on an assignment the instructions have to be read, not just a quick perusal, but a thorough examination. The mystery shopper should reflect on the instructions, think about whether they make sense and can be accomplished. The instructions should include a way to reach someone in case something goes wrong or a problem occurs. The number might not be toll free, but in this day and age of cell phones with long distance calling, contacting a non-toll-free number should not be a hardship.

When I perform assignments the first time I read the instructions before leaving the house, read them in the car before going in to shop, and reread them before leaving the area so I can be sure I've done what I am suppose to do. At least I try to do all this. I become careless if I've done the same shop several times. I think the instructions are not going to change. They sometimes do.

Those pesky instructions may include days and times jobs can be done. Usually there are reasons for dates and time. An office supply store cannot be shopped between certain hours because that is the time for inventory. The instructions may say to perform merchandising tasks between Tuesday and Friday. Monday is out because that is the day for restocking.

A lot of jobs will not be performed on the weekends, especially if they might interrupt customer sales during such a busy time. A few jobs may be done on Saturday or Sunday because it is intended to test whether employees can handle the crush of weekend traffic.

Food shops will call for specific shopping times based on what meal period the restaurants are testing. Might be breakfast, lunch, dinner, or a snack.

When mystery shopping at a restaurant find out what the rules are on times. Start times are usually clear. End times might mean that you have to be done with your meal and away from the building. Some restaurant shops only require that you have ordered your food before the end time. You can still be in or at the restaurant.

You will probably NOT get paid if you do not follow the instructions.

Keep Reading Those Instructions

I am being repetitive about instructions because they are the very reason you will get paid. For instance, I shopped two different well-known tax companies. One company has its own storefront; the other is located in a big box retailer. I was paid extremely well for the shops for one of the businesses and kind of okay pay for the other. These were multiple shops, which I am always thrilled with. I had to read the instructions very carefully for these shops because, of course, they were two different companies. I could have become complacent and just figured they were alike. They weren't.

I've walked out of stores without finishing my job because I didn't bother to read everything on the form I filled out in the store. Again, Yes or No answers — Is there a guide for the product on display? If the answer is yes then no picture is necessary. If the answer is no then take a picture of no guide on display. The request for the picture is clearly stated by the No answer I have circled. Did I see it? No. And I don't know I've missed a step until I fill out the report on my computer and the popup appears where the picture should be downloaded. Reread your forms before leaving an area, just like you reread the instructions.

One day I wandered through a big box retailer with instructions on exactly who to talk to – an employee wearing certain color clothing. I'd been assigned to a specific department. I'd wandered around for more than ten minutes without a single employee coming anywhere near me. Finally, someone comes along and says, "May I help you find something?"

My immediate reaction is relief. Someone who can help me complete my report. Then I look closely at the person and see they are wearing a red shirt. Red shirts are not good for this shop. Green shirts are called for. So I spend some time talking to the gal in the red shirt, but I can't use her information.

Well, I suppose I could use what she said, but that would be lying. And what if the form calls for her name? I put her name down from the nametag on the red shirt. Later, when someone representing the big box retailer reads the report, that someone has a list of employees working that day and the red-shirt employee was not one of those who could assist.

Revealed shops have forms you take in to the store. You put the forms on your clipboard and mark the answers as the manager responds or you inspect products.

Unrevealed shops are those where you make sure you do not show your forms to anyone. Again you will read through your forms and instructions before heading into a store.

Some mystery shopping companies have very exacting requirements for shops. You receive extensive information about how to conduct the shop and/or have to watch a video. Other companies have a list of shops, but the shopper has to read through a slide presentation and take a test. There may or may not be a limit to the number of times the test can be taken. Once the test is passed then access is available to the shops.

Probably there's more than the forms on the website, perhaps a page or two of instructions. Buried in those instructions is the fact you should take your Smartphone into the store. Now the report is to find out if the sales rep is knowledgeable about eprinting and what printer the rep would recommend for eprinting. Bringing the Smartphone means you talk about eprinting using that phone. Read everything!!!

Of course you have to have the Smartphone to begin with. By now you know what equipment you need to have but here's a reminder — computer, printer/scanner, digital camera, cellphone/Smartphone, and stopwatch or stopwatch app. The Smartphone might not be necessary, but it is helpful and would be necessary if you don't have a digital camera.

The Smartphone can be handy as a timing device. I still own a stopwatch, but it needs a battery. The Smartphone has a stopwatch app. When I did a shop at a fast food hamburger restaurant, the company included the information on how to access a different stopwatch app. I downloaded it and found the app had the ability to email the times recorded by the stopwatch to myself. I forwarded that email with the report thus providing a way to be sure I had read the times correctly.

Company Takeovers

The businesses running the mystery shops are as likely to change as the rules for a shop will change. Big companies gobble up smaller ones. Smaller companies lose contracts with businesses that have been clients for years and then cannot find a client that will produce similar income. Maybe the smaller business lasts for a few months, but then has to close down.

One day I received a lengthy email from an executive at a mystery shopping company being bought out by another mystery shopping company. The executive said the incoming group would contact the independent contractors who would be able to work for the new company. The hitch was that the contractors would need to fill out a form. The executive said to continue performing shops as we always had and that everything would work out. The forms would go out soon.

Now I've been hired and fired from "real" jobs, those where the taxes are taken out and someone made sure I worked forty hours a week or more. The email about the buyout shocked my system.

The email reminded me of my days working at a rural newspaper sold to new owners every three years. The new bosses would show up one day in suits and ties and everyone knew that we were in for life-changing experiences. Then I was one of about twenty employees. Now I was one of hundreds, probably even thousands, of people working for both companies. Probably not much would change. Everyone would have to go along with what would happen, but it would not be terribly traumatic since both companies were involved in mystery shopping.

Buyouts happen all the time and mystery shopping companies are not immune from everyday business occurrences.

Comparison Grocery Shopping

When the mystery shopper does comparison grocery shop, she takes a list of products into the store and finds the prices for those items. It's a simple task, except it makes me nervous. Nervous because I think someone will discover what I'm doing, create a scene, and unceremoniously throw me out of the store. I do have a vivid imagination, as you can tell.

The woman who hires me says that probably won't happen. She performs shops on the weekends for hundreds of items. She leads me to believe there should be no problems with this shop.

Yet when I walk into the store with my piece of paper I feel I'm wearing a sign on my back that says MYSTERY SHOPPER. One day my list consists of fifty items. My task is to not only find the prices, but also make sure I match the sizes. If I can't match then I write down the prices and sizes I do find. I'm supposed to be secretive and have a good story to tell if someone should ask what I am doing.

The first grocery comparison shop I did took two trips. It's a store my husband and I frequent for specific items. We don't shop there for everyday needs and walk all the aisles. I was familiar with the location of products we purchased. That meant I had to learn the location of other items and that took a very long time, two trips worth.

The second time I shopped this store I completed the task faster because I knew the location of more items. I'd increased my familiarity with product placement. I also noticed something that made me less nervous. The faces of employees had changed. With every shop in this store I notice a turnover in employees. I should not worry about someone recognizing me because the workers keep changing.

I also felt less awkward when I saw a woman carrying a clipboard with what appeared to be a grocery list. The clipboard made me feel a little bit better about my piece of paper. Yet I sometimes feel weird searching through the shelves, frozen food cabinets, and dairy bins for prices. Would someone come behind me and yell, "What are you doing? Why are you doing it? If you're mystery shopping you have to stop!"

That all assumed the people working in the store would have time between stocking and cashiering to register I was doing something weirder than checking my grocery list. Or that these same people, many who appeared new to the store, would know that people came in to write down prices for comparison purposes.

I also developed several scenarios I might use if someone questioned me. The one I practiced most often was the tale my sister taught a class of developmentally disabled students how to shop and cook. She didn't have time to check stores for prices because she was too busy teaching. I was retired and she'd convinced me to check the prices and write them down.

My other story was that I was taking my time and looking more closely at the items because I usually shopped with my husband. His idea of shopping is to get what we need and get out. I was taking my time because it was such a joy to be in the store without him. I was writing the prices so I could make a complete shopping list with the cost.

Don't Cheat. Don't Lie.

A bit of advice if you want to be a mystery shopper, don't cheat, don't lie. Simple advice that should be followed. I'm not talking about the pretend stories told to have a successful shop. I'm talking about the bigger picture.

I've tried to live without committing what can be called "little white lies" and especially without telling great big lies. Telling lies comes back to haunt a person. It's much too hard to keep track of lies that are told. Eventually a person trips and falls over those lies. The damage done may be major or minor, but there will be damage.

Don't cheat, lie, or pretend because you think that you won't be found out because the mystery shopping company is miles away. Who's going to check on what you do anyway? Or you think that.

Checking mechanisms exist for mystery shopping. Once you buy something in a store where you counted cartridges, toners, and photo papers then you should realize you are making that purchase to verify you were in the store.

There are people who would go to the store, make the purchase, and never perform the tasks required. It seems like so much more work to make up the information than checking the stock and answering the questions. It's harder to create a fictional report than to find the "real" information. Especially because there may be a trick question requiring a correct answer to get paid.

So don't pretend you've completed a shop when you haven't. Don't even think about lying about your job. Yes, it is a job. Don't tell yourself you can get away with pretending you've done your job when you haven't.

Don't sign off for a store manager because it's easier than finding the manager or any other excuse you can think of. You will probably not have a manager's name before you walk into a business, especially the first time in a store. You may need the manager's name to fill out your report. You may think you can get away with making up a name, but the report checkers may have a list of store managers and look up the names.

One time I misspelled a waitperson's name, not intentionally, an error on my part. I received a message asking me to check the name because the restaurant had no one by the name I had given working at the time I did the shop.

Some stores or restaurants have cameras on the property. Mystery shop forms may well warn the shopper of the cameras, straightforward stating not to lie or even stretch the truth because the cameras reveal the truth.

I don't lie because I'm afraid I'll get tangled up in those lies.

Why bother lying when all it gets you is being banned from working for the company you lied to and you aren't paid for the shop (a shop you spent a lot of time inventing)?

Tell Me A Story

You can, and often have to, pretend when mystery shopping. Pretending can be a major component of mystery shopping. When you enter a commercial establishment you are the customer, but you are often a customer with a specific mission, a mission set by the companies you work for. Note that I said companies because the mission you are on was selected by officials at the store where you are shopping and then handed on by your mystery shopping company.

You are shopping at a big box home improvement store. Your assignment is to enter the paint department and ask for help on a do-it-yourself project in your newly purchased townhouse. You have a specific list of questions to ask the department employee and then you are to leave, with the employee believing you will be back.

In reality you will not paint anything and do not live in a townhouse, but mystery shopping is composed of pretending in many cases. You will have to learn to be a decent actor. You're not going to win an Emmy or Golden Globe, but you'll earn your money and maybe help an employee do a better job for his employer and customers.

Sometimes I have to practice the story I'm going to tell. I practice because it may be way out of my realm of knowledge. One time I was in a big box retailer to scout out the backyard patio department. My task was to find an employee who could counsel me on creating a new patio. I had no clue about the details of building a patio so I started with simple basic questions which led to the other questions, like deciding how big to make the patio and calculating the needed materials.

Being inquisitive and enjoying talking to folks is important when mystery shopping and creating the stories that make your shop successful. When you talk to folks questions lead to answers, which lead to more questions, which lead to even more answers. Soon the conversation has covered what you need to report and you can disengage yourself politely to return to your vehicle and make notes that help you fill out your report once you reach your computer.

Instructions may include a basic outline for the story you use with more details than you can probably remember. Just do the best you can as you start out. The more detailed instructions may be based on what the employee is trained to do. Once you begin then the employee's responses will trigger your memory to recall the instructions.

Of course you already know better than to bring your paperwork into the store. And if you do bring it into the store then you should **not** pull it out of your pocket or purse to read while you talk to the employee. That is certainly not in your job description as a mystery shopper.

Writing The Narrative

Many mystery shops require a narrative, a story about what you did. Narratives are not difficult once you've done a few. Most mystery shopping companies provide examples of the narratives they need. If you follow the guidelines then you'll accomplish the job.

The guidelines provide the specific points to be addressed in the narrative. Perhaps the initial question is how the employees greeted you when you walked in and how quickly. Then there is a series of other actions and questions. You should jot down some notes when you get in your vehicle after you've done the shop. These can jog your memory.

Later you sit at your computer and think about the shop. Look at the example and see how much detail is expected before you start writing. Construct your answer like the example, but do not copy it exactly. Especially remember to use the name of the person involved in your mystery shop if that is required. Don't use the name in the example. You had your own experience.

Different companies have different narrative expectations. I had done several jobs for one outfit that requires a narrative. I wrote a lot of direct quotes from employees until I was told such were not needed. I could just write in general about what happened. That made my life a whole lot easier. I spent less time writing the report and the folks I reported to were just as happy.

Reports often ask for employee names. Employee descriptions can be very important, especially in circumstances where it is not possible to obtain names.

In cases where employees wear a nametag it's easy to provide a name, if the name on the tag is legible. There's sly ways to get people to tell you their name. I've used, "You look just like this woman I used to know named Tara." Most people's instinct when someone says that is to respond, "My name is Joanne." Once a woman said to me, "My name isn't Tara." I smiled sweetly and asked, "What is your name then?" Maybe she made up what she told me, but she gave me a name and that's what I used in the report.

Some companies do not want the shopper to ask for employee names. I had been shopping for a regional hamburger joint for several months. The employees I needed to identify always wore nametags. Then on one shop, the employee who took my order was not wearing a nametag.

I used my old standby of telling him he looked like someone I knew and he told me his name.

Now this particular company requires a complete narrative from walking in to leaving after eating the food. When I wrote the story of my shop I included the fact the employee had no nametag and that I had convinced him to tell me his name. Well, I was very surprised when I received the response that I should not try to get the name. My ploy could tell the employee I was a mystery shopper, which would impact on behavior.

So when I'm on my shops for this company I don't ask for employee names if they don't have a tag. I do concentrate on how to describe the employees — height, glasses or not, hair color, style hair, build. Some companies want ethnicity, other shy away from this part of a description. Once I find out a company's requisites for descriptions then I provide what they need.

Returning to the narrative, the directions for your shop will include instructions to make sure you spell words correctly and write in complete sentences. This is a serious request. The reports are not text messages with half phrases and letters for words. The reports are going on to the corporations that ordered them and must be understandable.

Paying For Travel

When I had a "real" job I was reimbursed for my travel, especially mileage. I spent many years working in the newspaper business. I sold advertising so I traveled the county visiting businesses. I learned early on that to be reimbursed I had to keep track of my mileage. I learned to look at the odometer in the car and write down the miles right after I started the vehicle.

Now I still do the same thing. As soon as I turn the engine on I grab my daybook, open it up to the current day, and write the mileage. A majority of the time I'm not going to get paid for my travel; however, I can write my mileage off against my income. But I know to do that I have to record the miles I travel every day while performing my tasks.

Writing the mileage is like any other habit. It takes time to become second nature. I also record the vehicle's use of gas and upkeep. I'm not an accountant (we have one for that reason), but keeping track of all this may not be useful unless you file a long form for your taxes. Check with a tax professional to find out.

I don't generally make special trips from my house to anywhere outside my immediate home area for mystery shops. I combine them with what I planned to do already or I take the shops on because they work in with whatever I am doing in a day. That's because the pay for shopping is not generally enough to cover the costs of the wear and tear on a vehicle plus gas. But if I am already planning on being in an area and there's a shop nearby, then I sign up for the shop.

Once in a while I am paid mileage, but that is a very special circumstance. I have been paid as much as 180 miles one way. I made the commitment to do the trip when a mystery shopping company representative called and asked if I would go if paid mileage. I tentatively agreed. I was shocked when the person asked me to tell him how much I would need to be paid. What an ingenious way for the company to save money! If they didn't make an offer then they didn't have to pay more than the agent was willing to take. If I say I want more than they are willing to spend then they can always turn me down.

One windy New Mexico morning an agent called to ask me to travel to a town I had never been to before to perform a business inspection. I stood outside in that wind trying to decide what my time, gas, and wear and tear on my vehicle were worth. I didn't want to overprice myself, but I didn't want to sell my services for cheap. I ran numbers frantically through my mind and came up with what I thought was a fair price. The agent waited patiently, but then he probably had plenty of practice. Undoubtedly he had done this bargaining before, and knew a smart shopper would take some time to come up with a "fair" number.

When I told the agent the amount he promptly said, "I'll check with my manager." I stood in a windy alcove and waited. Now I'll never know if he did check with a manager or if he already had some figures he could work with. When he came back on the line, he said the amount was fine.

Another time I was paid extra for driving fifty miles to and fifty miles back to buy a sandwich at a fast food restaurant. This restaurant had lingered on the to-be-shopped list for a long time. Guess the company had no shoppers in this town that was a long way from the "Big City." Again a mystery shopping company agent called me and asked how much I wanted to perform the shop. I underpriced myself on this one, but it wasn't a bad drive and I covered my vehicles expenses, if not necessarily my time.

Vendors Logs / Assignment Timing

Sometimes your shop will be called an audit. These are revealed shops. Audit is an acceptable word to most people, except when spoken by a representative of the Internal Revenue Service. I find it an easy word to say when a manager greets me at a big box office supply. I say I'm there to perform an audit on (pick a product in an office supply store). Usually the manager says that if I need any help I should call on him/her. Sometimes s/he asks me to sign a vendors log.

That word vendor. You are not selling anything, but the vendors log accounts for people coming through stores who are not customers or employees. A vendors log usually asks for your name, company you represent, time in, and time out. Some stores may add a space for the task performed. Often you sign in when you start the job and then you sign out when you finish. I've taken the easy way and signed the in and out when I sign in because I'm bound to forget to sign out. I'll waltz my way out the exit and be gone with no thought of leaving a departure time by the arrival time I'd signed twenty-five minutes earlier.

Not all stores have a log, not all managers ask mystery shoppers to sign the log. A mystery shopping company may tell you to sign the vendors log. I've done jobs where my instructions explicitly say sign the vendors log. I don't know if a vendors log will hold up in court, but evidently mystery shopping companies consider it reliable enough to insist on a signature with the other pertinent information.

Mystery shoppers can become well known to store employees if the shoppers go into a store more often than would be normal. Stores will have a set number of days between visits for shoppers. I worked for one company that had a year between shops at stores.

Some companies require two months between visits. The furniture company's year seems excessive. Managers and employees may have a good enough memory to recognize a shopper if they are in their store too frequently, but a couple months seems enough time not to be recognized as a shopper.

With computer systems it's easy to keep track of visits. I visited bedding shops for one mystery shopping company. There are more than fifteen shops across our metropolitan area. I forget when I last visited different shops, but the computer doesn't. If I try signing up for a shop before my sixty days have passed, the computer will tell me I need to wait.

Spending Your Money

Most mystery shopping jobs require the shopper spend money. This is especially true of food shops. Often the instructions say that the shopper is to use cash, especially at fast food restaurants. Although debit, and even credit, cards can be used to make purchases, cash is frequently handed over. Employees have to know how to make change, even if the cash register tells you what the change is.

The cash register can tell the employee that the charge is $8.61, the customer gives the employee a $10 bill, and the change is $1.39. Yet the biggest consideration is that the employee can handle the buttons on the register and knows what money looks like. Well, cash registers no longer have buttons. It's more like pressing a key. But if I order a hot dog with relish and onions then the employee has to know what to push to create the receipt and send the order to the people cooking.

When I finish ordering then the total must be rung up on the register. The customer has to be told how much they need to pay so the employee has to read the numbers on the register. When I hand over the money then the employee has to know how to ring up the amount I gave her and give me the correct change, if necessary.

Cash registers have taken away the task of figuring how to make change to some degree, but those at the register have to know how to count out that change. In a register emergency they should know how to actually make change, usually by writing down the numbers on paper.

I've used credit cards on some shops, usually ones that involve more than ten dollars. I've mystery shopped at casual restaurants where the average bill, with tip, for two is twenty-five to thirty dollars. I don't carry that much cash, and, if I did, I'd rather put that charge on my card.

The credit card receipt is not what you generally send when you make the report. The restaurant listing of what you ordered, including drinks, should be sent, especially if the shop instructions calls for two different entrees. Two different entrees meant just that – a hamburger and salad, steak and chicken. Two different entrees does not mean two hamburgers – one with mushrooms, one naked, both with a bun. The object of ordering two different entrees is to know whether the chefs can cook various items. Ordering different entrees can be mandatory. Ordering the same entrée for each person can mean not getting paid for the job including the tip.

Save the receipt that lists the entrees and other items you ordered since that's the one you will send with your report, even if you paid with a credit card. And don't lose any of your receipts, even when you get home, especially if you are taking the expenses off your taxes so you can offset the income you receive from your shopping.

Mystery shops can be fun and rather exotic and lots more expensive than a fast food restaurant. National Parks with hotels and restaurants need to be evaluated to be sure customers receive adequate care and attention. Imagine a partially-paid-for-by-someone-else four-day trip to a National Park. Partially paid because the tab that is picked up is the hotel stay, breakfast and dinner for two, and purchases in hotel gift shops.

Sounds magnanimous, doesn't it, especially if the hotel room costs $200 a night and a dinner for two is $150. But other expenses have to be factored into the equation of mystery shopping at a National Park or resort area — the travel to the site, lunch, the not-to-be refunded money you spent on items you just had to have.

Those items not reimbursed can include that third drink when you are paid for ordering two and paying with cash to check the handling of money. You might not get your money back for the third cute potholder you bought when your total expense was $15 in the gift shop and you were told you'd be compensated $10 for finding out how the cashier handles cash.

Smile, You're On Candid Camera

A popular television show years back was *Smile, You're On Candid Camera*. The show has been reincarnated a few times so you may have seen it in one form or another. The premise was that people would do just about anything and that just about anything could be filmed and replayed for a television audience.

You're not filming a scene for *Candid Camera*, but you do have to know how to take pictures for a variety of shops. Some food shops require a picture of the meal. I've ordered my food to eat in the restaurant from the counter area where it is served. I bring the food to my table. Before I begin eating, my task is to photograph everything.

The instructions offer suggestions for explaining why I'm taking the picture if anyone should ask. I'm taking the pictures for a friend who misses this particular type of food. Really? Seems to me my friend would not want to see such a picture because it would just make her hungry for something she evidently could not have. Another reason, say my instructions, is that I put pictures of everything I eat on my website or Facebook.

I pull out my Smartphone, stand up, and focus the camera on the food, drink, utensils, and napkins (I'm thorough if nothing else), and snap the picture as unobtrusively and quickly as I can. I want to look around and see if someone is watching me, but I don't. That would probably be more obvious then just sitting down and starting to eat.

During the summer I shopped for a hamburger and sundae at a well-known fast food restaurant. Again, part of the shop was taking a picture of the food. Two pictures, one of the hamburger and one of the sundae. I conducted the shop on a very hot dusty New Mexico late afternoon. I couldn't ask for a cover for the sundae because it might smoosh the topping. While the hamburger cooked, the woman behind the counter fixed my sundae and handed it to me. Oh, my, it started melting immediately even though I stood in an air-conditioned building.

I silently wished someone would call my number indicating my hamburger was ready. Finally, my number came up. I grabbed the bag with the hamburger, slammed the door open, and rushed across the parking lot. Actually, I rushed as fast as I could because I feared if I ran then the ice cream might melt faster. I reached the car, threw the hamburger bag across to the passenger seat, put the sundae on the console, dragged my Smartphone from my purse, and shot a picture of the sundae before it melted into its plastic cup. I took a picture of the hamburger and then ate the sundae first.

A multiple shop I did involved three tasks at one fast food restaurant. I started with purchasing a relatively inexpensive piece of food. I timed the delivery of the food. I had a list of questions the employee was supposed to ask me. Once I consumed that food then I returned to the counter and told the employee whether they would be rewarded ten dollars or had to improve their presentation.

I hate having to present the employee with the news they will not get an extra reward. Employees who receive ten dollars cash are ecstatic. Wouldn't you be if you were working for minimum wage? A ten-dollar bill would look great.

The bosses also seemed appreciative when I gave their employee the money. Maybe the boss receives extra money in her paycheck for training the employee so well.

The third task was photographing the menu and various signs in the restaurant. I performed a similar assignment for other fast food restaurants.

The business verification for one company involved many pictures. The instructions specifically stated using a digital camera. To me that means a camera, not a phone. Some shop instructions say a Smartphone can be used. Some people might consider a Smartphone a digital camera. I have a digital camera and I use it for shops, especially the ones that require a multiple of photographs, even three to five photos.

I use my Smartphone periodically to photograph receipts so I can turn in my reports from places other than my home office where I have a scanner. If I know I'm going to fill out a report on the road then I usually photograph the receipt on the console of my vehicle.

Smartphones have as much, if not more, capabilities as digital cameras. I think I understand the insistence by some companies on using digital cameras. Not all phone cameras are alike, especially earlier generations. Easier to say in the instructions that digital cameras must be used. Some shoppers will go ahead and use a Smartphone, figuring that no one will know the difference.

Some tasks involve taking pictures only if something is not correct. The question may be "Is there a display of five different cell phones near the cash register?" The answer is Yes or No. If you answer No then the instruction is to take a picture. You pull out your camera or Smartphone to take a photo of where the five phones are supposed to be but there are only three. Maybe the employees have not noticed that someone swiped the phones. Or maybe the phones never came in.

Once you have the photos in your camera or Smartphone you need to download them to your computer and then send them. Most cameras and Smartphones have the cords that connect between the picture-taking device and the computer. And once everything is connected and turned on it is usually fairly simple to download the pictures. My system asks me if I want to delete the photos from the camera or Smartphone once the pictures are downloaded. In my fear that the computer has eaten the pictures before they show up on the system, I usually keep the pictures on the device. That means that eventually, probably months later, I remove them. Some cameras transmit to computers wirelessly now.

I try to be unobtrusive when I take pictures. No reason to call attention to myself. I've rarely been asked what I'm doing. One day a man pleasantly asked why I was taking photos of the shopping center where he had his business.

"I'm doing a property inspection," I responded. I then gave him the name of a woman to call if he had any questions.

"Oh, that's my landlady. Sure. Okay." He wandered away as quickly as he appeared.

Collecting Cards and Brochures

Most mystery shopping involves no extra items. You order your food, pay for it, eat it on site, take your receipt, and return home to make your report. Some reports require extra information. One of the items on the list for business verifications is asking for brochures or business cards. I ask, and most of the time I end up taking away business cards. Sometimes I walk out with fancy brochures or a stack of information a quarter inch thick that I can't use. Then I feel guilty.

All the time and expense to put together a sales pitch and I'm not interested enough to read through it. All I care about is scanning the cover. I hang on to the stuff the requisite ninety days and then I throw it out.

Same with the business cards. I scan them and attach the jpeg to the proper place in the report and staple the cards to my hard copy to save until I feel safe recycling all the paper I've accumulated from my shops.

I do recycle most of the paper. Some things I shred because I don't think they are anyone's business but mine. But at least I make myself feel good by recycling most of the paper produced when mystery shopping. Mystery shopping companies tell you how long you should keep information, especially the receipt. A lot of them are ninety days. I leave the scans in my computer for a couple months.

It was almost the end of March when I received an email looking for a fast food receipt from early February. Out of curiosity, I went onto their website and checked their records. I saw that the requested receipt had been downloaded and even approved. The receipt was still in my computer's Mystery Shopping file. Rather than questioning their request, I wrote a note saying I was sending the receipt jpeg and sent it. Sometimes things are not worth arguing about or expending extra energy saying, "You say you have this."

Checking Out The Facilities

Part of the mystery shop in many restaurants is inspecting the bathroom. Note that I didn't say bathrooms. Mystery shoppers are not expected to inspect the bathroom for the opposite sex. I shopped a popular fast food restaurant for months. I never looked for or asked about a bathroom. Then the instructions changed and asking became important. If there was a public restroom then inspecting it was part of the job.

The instructions to inspect public restrooms began appearing several weeks before shoppers had to perform the task. The instruction was included in every piece of information about the shop, pointing out this would be a requirement with the start date.

Then the question became a task for the shop. The first time I had to do a bathroom inspection I did remember to ask about the restroom before I left the fast food parking lot.

Don't avoid the restrooms if they are part of the job and are accessible. Make sure you check them out.

When Businesses Shut The Doors

The instructions for shops often include what to do when a store is no longer in business. I had done many shops before I was assigned one where the restaurant had closed. I was very surprised when I drove up to the corner of the shopping center where the store had been for years and realized all the signs with the restaurant name had been taken down.

I got out of the car and walked up to the door to read a note that said the restaurant was permanently closed. I didn't remember the instructions for what to do if the facility was no longer operating and the information was not part of what I had printed out and taken with me. I did pull my camera from the car to take pictures of the closed restaurant, including photographing the note on the door and a shot of the restaurant part of the shopping center showing the overhead exterior signs had been totally removed. I included the address of the building in the pictures when I could because addresses are always important in mystery shopping.

Once I settled back home at my computer I sent an email to the company that assigned me the job. The email included the information the store had closed and a photo of the front of the restaurant showing the address. The response was a reminder that the instructions did say what to do if a restaurant was closed, but I had covered everything that needed to be done.

Maybe I should be surprised that more businesses I had been assigned had not closed as the country went through tough economic times. But this was the only one I found in my work.

This Could Be Scary

I haven't worked much retail nor have I been behind the counter in fast food restaurants, but I know that people walk into stores and restaurants to rob what cash there might be. I was in a fast food restaurant the morning a man demanded all the money the employee could produce.

I was eating my food in a booth that Saturday morning. The restaurant hadn't been that busy in the fifteen minutes I'd been there. I watched a few people come in, order, get their food, and leave. I didn't pay much attention to a short skinny man who entered until he ordered a hamburger. It was before eight in the morning so that request seemed odd. I turned my attention back to my food, but soon noticed the man run out of the store. Only a few seconds later an employee yelled, "We've just been robbed!"

Employees came from other areas of the store to lock doors and call 911. One of the employees looked straight at me and said, "I'm sorry you had to be here for this."

I waited in my corner of the restaurant for the police to arrive, figuring I was a witness. The first officer looked over at me when she walked through. She asked if I had been there and I said "yes." I offered to stay, but she said I could go. As I was heading out the door, another officer entered. She asked if anyone had talked to me. I said "no" so she asked me to give what information I could. I gave the officer my name, phone number, and my version of the events. I walked out of the restaurant and when I settled in my car I felt tremendous relief. I had been very scared.

Then my brain let loose with a hundred thoughts and I began shaking. What if the robber had been a real crazy and began shooting up the restaurant? Sure, there weren't that many people in the place. But did that matter to a psycho? What if the robber had taken all of us hostage? What if the robber was waiting around the restaurant to see what happened and would jump into my car? I quickly made sure my doors were locked, just in case.

I have no clue as to how many mystery shoppers might be

somewhere close by when a robbery occurs. There's no way of knowing when to stay clear of a place because it's going to be robbed. Employees can't anticipate a robbery so how will shoppers? My best advice is to be careful when it happens. Don't be a hero, or heroine in my case. Don't be foolish. It could get you killed.

The Bad and Strange Shops

The reasons mystery shopping is important should be evident – to make sure shoppers have a good experience. One bad experience can send a customer away forever.

I detest giving bad reviews when writing up mystery shops. If there is something bad about my experience then I try to find something good that happened. But the bad has to be written about because that's why we are paid to mystery shop.

One day I ate a mystery shop lunch at a burger joint that's well liked in the Southwestern United States. I had never eaten a bad meal at this chain. Then I tasted a meal so bad that I threw out half the food without finishing it.

I knew I would have to report the bad food but I hesitated. I called the scheduler and asked, "I had an awful meal at my assignment today. Do I report it?"

"Of course," she responded. "That's why you're doing this. To tell people something is wrong so it can be fixed."

She explained that the shops (the assignment was the same for several restaurants) might have been created because restaurant management had received reports that particular food had problems. The way to find out if this was true was to mystery shop the specific meal.

I was brutally honest making my report, revealing that both the French fries and iced tea tasted good, but I couldn't finish the meal because the meat's odd flavor tainted my taste buds.

During a shop at a bedding store, the manager excused herself to help a woman buy travel pillows. The manager told me we would finish our business after she sold the woman the pillows. She and I both figured it would be a quick sale. Not at all.

The new customer chattered on for several minutes about saving the planet as she refused to give the manager her address for the sale. The manager then had to figure out a way around her computer system that called for an address. The simple transaction took longer than I or the manager thought it would or should. The manager was very tactful dealing with the woman. I found this so impressive that I mentioned what happened in my report.

Others might not have found it important to talk about, but the new customer put the pressure on the manager by taking up a lot of time. The manager handled the customer and me in a way that she made the pillow sale and she would have sold me if I had really been interested in buying a new mattress.

Mistakes I Have Made

When I perform a new shop, at a place I've never been before, I try to do it perfectly. Ha! If it's an unrevealed shop, one where I have to remember details, then my chances of perfection are somewhat slim. I probably will not make a major mistake, but I will forget something. When I sit in my vehicle to check my papers before leaving then the error of my ways slaps me in the face. Sometimes I can fix what I mess up. Sometimes I confess I did something wrong and beg for forgiveness from the manager of the store where I've made the mistake.

What appeared to be a simple task turned out to be about the biggest mistake I made in my mystery shopping career. It happened at a big box retailer. It happened after I had been performing shops for several years. But I had not done this type of job and the instructions were minimal.

My job was to install the signage for Back To School clothes. I didn't have to unpack and stock the clothing. Store employees did that. The labels and signs would be shipped to me. I would bring those to the store. A big box arrived at the house about a week before the first job. Turned out it was a three-part task, divided up into different clothing. The instruction said to take down the old signage and put up the new. The signs were attractive and advertised the different fall styles of an assortment of women's, children's, and men's clothing.

I had performed a variety of jobs at this big box retailer and knew that I could avoid the hordes of people who shopped there by working in the morning. The earlier in the morning, the fewer people. I generally liked to get there between half past eight and nine. The employees seemed to be organized by then and were still friendly.

The first morning I carried my big box of materials into the store and loaded it into a shopping cart. I made a point of talking to the woman who oversaw the cashiers about what I was doing that day. She gave me the names of the women working in the clothing area and said to talk to them before starting. Then I signed into the vendors log.

I pushed my cart over to women's clothing and searched out the department employees. When I found them I told them about my task. They had already received word that I would be there (not unusual as many store managers tell employees when jobs are scheduled to be performed by non-employees). They said they would be around if I had questions or needed help. Then they wandered off.

I checked my instructions, which said I needed to take down any signage before putting up the new signage. I started stripping off ALL the signage on the shelves of clothing and dumping it into a second shopping cart. Stripping off that signage proved no easy task. The plastic, which contained different numbers (numbers I didn't know the significance of at that point), seemed glued to the shelf edge. I was convinced this plastic was the signage I was supposed to remove. And so I did.

I blissfully pulled off the plastic before dipping into the cardboard box where I found plastic holders and the lightweight cardboard signs that went inside the holders. The holders would be attached to the shelves by little pins with the plastic and cardboard hanging below. The intent had been to place the holders with their cardboard signs over the plastic I had stripped off. That plastic with its numbers was the mechanism the employees used to place items on the shelves. I should not have pulled this particular plastic off the shelves.

Needless to say, the employees were not happy with me and I was very embarrassed. I had two more similar tasks to perform – one in the men's department and the second in the children's. I did not pull off that very important numbering system. I accepted being chastised gently by the employees for not checking with them before proceeding with my actions.

The signage I should have removed was from a previous installation and was easy to pull. I should have known by how difficult it was to pull that plastic that it wasn't the correct item to remove. When I knew about my mistake I looked back at the instructions. Nothing there indicated my decision on signage had been wrong. I just hadn't asked because I assumed I knew what I was doing. I didn't.

And a sidenote: the instructions for my second task had more explanation and pictures of what signage should be removed and the plastic replacements. Had these been included with the first job I don't think I would have made the mistakes I did. Mystery shopping is a continual learning process.

Most of my other errors were not so disastrous for folks' workloads. I've periodically driven to the wrong address. One time I drove to the wrong address with my husband along. Having him there seemed to magnify my error although I was only about a half mile from where I needed to be.

When I started mystery shopping I made minor mistakes and most of them I could fix relatively painlessly. One mistake I didn't make for several years was to be uncovered as a mystery shopper. The one time I was discovered was at a shoe store where I can no longer mystery shop because my computer doesn't work with the company forms.

When I performed my original shop, I looked for a specific style shoe. The manager found a pair and explained that the store had many of them. She had no idea why she had been sent so many, but kept them knowing they were a style that would eventually be purchased. I reported what she said when I sent my form in and gave her high marks for the way she handled herself and the sale.

A few months later, I returned to purchase one of those many pair. When I walked up to the counter to conclude my purchase the woman waited on me again. She asked me if I had found everything and I responded with a "You did such a good job the last time I was here I had no problems. You told me where to find these shoes."

The woman's eyes grew bright and she just about screeched, "You're my secret shopper!"

I admitted I was saying, "Yes, I am. But I'm not now. The company changed its forms and I can't do that form."

I don't think she even heard me. She appeared thrilled to identify me. I suppose she received compliments for my report, maybe even a raise in her salary. I didn't feel bad she had discovered me because I was no longer performing shops for the company. And she made me feel good showing such enthusiasm to a stranger.

After I concluded my purchase, she said, "I have to give you a hug." She came around the counter and hugged me.

There are other ways to recognize a mystery shopper. The bedding store I've shopped is usually a one-person operation so I have seen some store managers more than once or twice. I don't think there is anything special about me that makes me recognizable. However I have had experiences in two different stores.

I walked into one bedding store with a manager I had met on a shop at a different location miles away. He welcomed me to the store and then said, "Haven't you been in here before? You look familiar."

I had been in the store before, but not when he was there. I had been there when a woman was running the store, a woman who complimented me on my shoes. I carefully avoided wearing the same shoes, thinking she would be there and remember them. (Yes, they were that distinctive.)

My response when he said I looked familiar was "Oh, you know, all senior citizen blondes look alike. I probably look like a lot of people who come in here."

This seemed to satisfy him, but I was very surprised when the manager of another bedding store said, "That's a beautiful necklace. Have you been in here before? I seem to remember it."

Some of my jewelry is very distinctive, probably one of a kind, and I forget that. Everyone has his or her own particular interests. This woman's might have been jewelry since she was wearing a very nice necklace herself.

"Thanks for the compliment," I said, fingering the necklace. "I've seen women wearing similar designs."

She accepted that explanation and we proceeded with the mattress demonstration. But I became very careful about what jewelry I wear when I mystery shop. In fact, I often take off my jewelry before going into a store.

Sometimes I feel my secret has been revealed even though I have done nothing more than act like any other customer. An employee will do just exactly as they are supposed to do, for instance come by with a condiment tray and ask if I need anything, and I think "Wow, do they know I'm mystery shopping and checking their actions?" Then my brain says, "No, they are doing their job."

While my sister was sick I didn't do much mystery shopping. Once she started recovering I took on some jobs. One day I went to an office supply store, checked out the cartridges, toners and photo papers, made a cheap purchase to prove I'd been in the store, and left. I chose not to make my report that same day as the shop because I didn't have access to a scanner.

The next day when I reported the shop and emailed my scanned receipt I was informed my pay would be reduced because I had not reported within the correct time frame. This was my mistake. I did know better, but I had forgotten. Shops need to be reported in a timely fashion and/or as required. I could have photographed the receipt, saved it to my computer, and sent it in that format. I wasn't going to be paid that much to begin with for the job. The small amount became even less.

Final Words

Mystery shopping is not for everyone and it definitely won't get you rich. Mystery shopping may pay very poorly. I received a check in the mail (yes, in the mail) for a grand total of $13.94. That magnanimous sum was for 90 minutes of work plus 42 cents of printing. The job was inventorying DVDs at a variety store except I had not just inventoried. I had also moved the DVDs into their correct display case. It was mindless physical work with a bit of thought when inventorying.

When I performed the job it was after a buyout. The company I'd done this for sold out to another mystery shopping company. I'd worked a deal for the first company to pay me $11 an hour. The new company only paid $8 and only paid for ninety minutes, even if the job took longer. That's what their paperwork clearly said.

When the first company paid me it was usually lumped in with other jobs and I didn't really examine how much I received for individual tasks. That $13.94 check makes me wonder about my sanity performing jobs I travel to after spending time reading instructions. People are earning $8 an hour in everyday jobs and I think that it is just not enough money.

Timing can be important in mystery shopping and time can be elusive. Give yourself enough time to get the job done, but not so much that you are losing money. And watch the times on the instructions. And once more I'll emphasize that you need to read the instructions very carefully and follow them even more carefully.

Mystery shopping can be fun but the shopper can be abused. But then it is the shopper's choice taking on jobs and s/he has to learn to pick and chose the jobs that will satisfy them.

I took on a shop at a party items store. The store has a great selection of anything and everything for a party or get-together with much of it in matching designs. The employees were super helpful and seemed to be everywhere. Trouble was that I had no interest in just about anything the store sold. It took me way too long to find something to buy so I could get a receipt and prove I'd been in the shop. The something I selected is still on the shelf. There's no sense performing a shop that pays the standard mystery shop rate if one doesn't find something to buy that's useful or cute or somewhat fun. I haven't taken a shop at this store since my first and only opportunity to scour through the inventory.

I, and you, don't have to take a shop unless you want to. Maybe you like the food at a particular fast food restaurant and you have the contacts to get shops there. That makes sense. Maybe the fees are greatly increased at a fast food restaurant you are not particularly fond of. You take the shop because the money is good. If you find you don't like a store or restaurant don't feel obligated to take another shop there unless it's absolutely something you want to do.

Mystery shopping is something different to do and can earn a bit of gas money. Be careful what jobs you take on. Not all of them will be pleasing to everyone, and some can be more fun than others. When you do a job, follow the instructions, fill out the reports, and send the receipts.